A TASTE OF IRELAND

A TASTE OF IRELAND

IRISH TRADITIONAL FOOD

BY THEODORA FITZGIBBON

Period photographs specially prepared by George Morrison

AVENEL BOOKS · NEW YORK

For EDWARD MORRISON with affection

ACKNOWLEDGMENTS

I wish to thank the friends who have helped me in my research, particularly Mrs Alice Beary for the loan of eighteenth-century family manuscripts, from which the endpapers are taken, and my aunt, Mrs Roberta Hodgins, Clonlara, Co. Clare.

My thanks are also due to Dr A. T. Lucas, Director of The National Museum of Ireland, for giving me access to his paper *Irish Food before the Potato*, and to The National Library of Ireland for their help with books, manuscripts and photographs.

CONTENTS

viii

INTRODUCTION

The descendants of many of the people depicted in these pages are now scattered all over the world. Some have achieved renown in many ways: as poets, publicans or presidents. It is on some of these foods that their ancestors were nourished.

Irish stew, Limerick ham, corned beef and cabbage are well-known everywhere, but as there are traditional dishes in many European countries which have been forgotten, so Ireland is no exception.

The best food of a country is the traditional food which has been tried and tested over the centuries. It suits the climate, and uses the best products of that country. This is borne out by the superb classical cuisine of France, which has changed very little with the years.

Fashion alters food habits as much as it alters dress. Two or three hundred years ago in Ireland the food was, in a way, more imaginative than it is today: especially in the use of vegetables. Globe artichoke bottoms (spelt Harty Choake in old manuscripts) were used for stuffings as well as a vegetable. Nowadays they are thought a luxury, and yet they grow freely here. Charlock (*Sinapis arvensis*), not unlike spinach, now regarded as a weed, was eaten a lot in the eighteenth and nineteenth centuries. Caleb Threlkeld, writing in *Synopsis stirpium Hibernicarum*, 1727, says: 'It is called about the streets of Dublin before the Flowers blow, by the name of Corn-cail, and used for boiled sallett.' Sea-kale, that most delicate of winter vegetables, was known as Strand cabbage in Donegal, and served like asparagus, with melted butter (drawn butter). Carrots were made into a pudding with spices, eggs, breadcrumbs and butter: in literature they have been called 'honey underground'. Leeks, many forms of onion, and particularly garlic are found in the earliest sources as a flavouring as well as a food. An early poem says:

Is leighas air gach tinn	*(Garlic with May butter*
Cheamb 'us im a Mhàigh	*Cureth all disease*
Ol 'an flochair sid	*Drink of goat's white milk*
Bainne-ghobhar bán.	*Take along with these.)*

These were eaten before the potato, which was to play such a significant part in the country's history, was introduced by Sir Walter Raleigh in 1585, and planted on his estate in County Cork.

The recipes in this book have been drawn from all sections of Irish life, both rural and urban: many are still cooked daily, as all the ingredients are readily available; others are familiar names, and seldom appear outside private homes. The food of a country is part of its history and civilization, and, ideally, the past and the present should be combined, so that traditional food is not lost under a pile of tins or packages.

We, in Ireland, have long memories: the aromas from the kitchens of our childhood remain when many other things are forgotten. I hope that this little book will revive those memories and bring pleasure to all who use it.

THEODORA FITZGIBBON, 1968

Deilginis   Dalkey
Baile Átha Cliath   Dublin

A NOTE FOR AMERICAN READERS

Since your oven, whether gas or electric, is calibrated in degrees Fahrenheit, you can ignore the gas-oven recommendations given in the recipes and rely on the indicated temperatures. Irish ovens are calibrated in a different way.

A TASTE OF IRELAND

KIDNEYS IN THEIR OVERCOATS

A popular breakfast dish in the early years of the century, and still the way to get the most flavour from lambs' kidneys.

The kidneys are cooked in a hot oven in their jacket of fat. This ensures that all the juices are there, and also that they are not overcooked. They make an excellent luncheon dish, served on dry toast, with jacket-boiled potatoes and freshly cooked spinach.

Take 2 to 3 kidneys per person, depending on the size. Put the kidneys with their case of fat into a baking dish and cook in a pre-heated oven (400° F. electric; gas regulo 6) for 30 minutes, or until the fat is crisp and melted. Break open when put on toast, and serve with salt and pepper. A little of the crisp fat is good when eaten with the boiled potatoes.

City Hall, Dublin, 1858. Daniel O'Connell Statue

POTATO SOUP

Traditional: Roberta Colbert, Cloughjordan, Co. Offaly (b. 1884).

2 lb. potatoes
2 oz. (2 heaped tablesp.) butter
3 pts. (6 cups) of half milk and water or stock and milk
chopped chives or parsley

2 medium-sized onions
1 cup light cream
6 rashers streaky bacon, crisply fried
salt and pepper

Melt the butter in a saucepan, add the sliced and peeled onions and cook gently. Do not let them brown. Add the peeled and sliced potatoes, season to taste, then pour over the milk and water or stock. Cover and cook gently for about an hour. It is then sieved or put into a liquidizer until it is puréed. Add the cream and gently re-heat, but do not boil. Serve with freshly chopped chives or parsley on top, and the crisply fried bacon rashers finely broken up with a fork, as a garnish.

This soup can also be made with leeks instead of onions. Additional garnishes instead of bacon are chopped Dublin Bay prawns or small dice of lobster.

Kilkenny, Co. Kilkenny, c. 1908

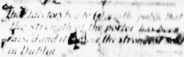

PORTER CAKE

Margaret Saunders, Carrick-on-Suir, Co. Tipperary (b. 1875).

Porter was a weak form of stout or Guinness. Nowadays it is not made, but Guinness is used for this recipe, which makes an excellent moist and rich cake.

1 lb. (4½ cups) sifted cake flour
1 lb. (2½ cups) brown sugar
1 lb. (3 cups) seedless raisins [1]
½ lb. (1½ cups) sultanas
1 level teasp. bicarbonate of soda, melted in warm Guinness
4 eggs
½ lb. (1 cup) butter
4 oz. (1 cup) glacé cherries
4 oz. (1 cup) blanched chopped almonds
4 oz. (1 cup) mixed chopped peel
½ pt. Guinness, warmed
juice and grated rind of 1 lemon
pinch of mixed spice

Rub the butter into the flour and add all the other dry ingredients. Blend very well. Beat the eggs with the lukewarm Guinness and add the bicarbonate of soda. Mix this very well into the dry cake mixture, and turn into a greased and lined cake tin, measuring 9 in. in diameter and 3 in. high. It should be covered with a greaseproof paper, and baked in a slow oven (200° F.–250° F. electric; gas regulo ½–1) for about 3–3½ hours, removing the paper for the last half-hour. Test with a skewer before removing from the oven. It makes a good Christmas cake, and if iced will keep well in a tin.

[1] Half currants and half raisins can be used if preferred.

SALAD DRESSING

Ellen Allen, Ballinrig, Co. Meath (1840–1917).

2 hard-boiled eggs
1 dessertsp. (2 teasp.) malt vinegar

2 teasp. each of dry mustard and sugar
½ pt. (1 cup) sour cream, or fresh cream with the juice of half a lemon dripped in and stirred

Pound the eggs and dry ingredients together until well blended. Then add the vinegar and sour cream gradually. Tear apart the lettuce and put into salad bowl. When the dressing is smooth, pour over, and serve at once. This dressing can also be used over cooked sliced beetroot, raw chicory or endive and shredded cabbage. More sugar can be added to taste if desired. The cream originally used was just slightly soured; it was brought from the dairy and left by a hot stove until it thickened.

The *Illustrated London News* of 1867 remarks on the excellence and delicious taste of Kerry butter. Caherciveen was the market centre for it. The following is from *A Sportsman in Ireland* by A Cosmopolite, 1897:

'I then visited the Market House at Killarney, which was well supplied with abundance of sea-fish and meat. The prices were as follows: pork 2d per pound; beef 3d to 3½d; mutton 4d; codfish 6 lb. 1/–; fowls 10d a pair; chickens from 6d–6½d; potatoes 4½d per stone; salmon 4d per pound and a goodly mass of arbutus [strawberry tree, *Arbutus unedo*, which has a bright red berry not unlike a strawberry to look at, but disappointing to taste] fruits which are indigenous to this part of Kerry.'

In the grounds of the Lake Hotel, Killarney, Co. Kerry, 1867

BOILED FRUIT CAKE

Patricia Thorne, Birdhill, Co. Tipperary.

1 lb. (2½ cups) sultanas   ½ lb. (1 cup) butter or margarine
½ lb. (1 cup) granulated sugar   ¼ pt. (½ cup) water
1 teasp. mixed spice

Boil the above ingredients for 10 minutes, mixing well. Let it get cold, then add:

1 lb. (4½ cups) sifted flour   2 well-beaten eggs

Blend very well, then put the mixture into a greased and lined cake tin (8 in. in diameter) and bake in a slow oven (250° F. electric; gas regulo ½–1) for about 2 hours.

This is a good moist cake which keeps very well. Chopped nuts may be added if liked.

DUBLIN ROCK

A rich, decorative pudding of the 1880s and 1890s. It must have looked very ornate on the long dining-tables of the period.

4 oz. ($\frac{1}{2}$ cup) butter or 1 cup very thick cream
2 stiffly beaten egg whites
a few drops of orange flower water

$\frac{1}{2}$ lb. (2 cups) ground almonds
2 oz. ($\frac{1}{4}$ cup) caster sugar
1 tablesp. brandy
angelica, blanched split almonds and maidenhair fern for decoration

Make an earthenware mixing bowl very hot, and into it put the butter or cream. Beat into this the almonds and sugar, and when well mixed add the brandy and a few drops of orange flower water. (This can usually be bought at a chemist.) The beating should continue until the bowl is quite cold, then the stiffly beaten egg whites are added and well amalgamated (nowadays this could all be done in an electric blender). The mixture is then left overnight in a cold place until it is quite stiff. It is then broken into rough pieces (it will be soft but firm) and piled on to a glass dish in the shape of a pyramid.

It is decorated with strips of green angelica, shredded blanched almonds and, in the old days, little fronds of maidenhair fern to resemble plants, such as shamrock, growing out of a rock.

In England it was known as Irish Rock, and when pineapples were a novelty in the nineteenth century, the mixture was often shaped to resemble one, spiked with almonds and garnished round the base with crystallized fruits.

St Stephen's Green, Dublin, c. 1860

BOXTY

'Boxty on the griddle, Boxty in the pan,
If you don't eat Boxty you'll never get a man.'

Boxty is a traditional Irish potato dish served on the eve of All Saints' Day, All Hallows' Eve (see also pages 67 and 69). Boxty on the griddle resembles griddle cakes and Boxty in the pan is a kind of potato bread. Mr Patrick Gallagher, born in Cleendra, Co. Donegal, in 1873, and known as 'Paddy the Cope' (Cope being a mispronunciation of Co-op) as he was the principal founder of the Templecrone Co-operative Society in 1906, recalled just before his death in 1966, at the age of ninety-two, that when he was a child Boxty was often served instead of oat bread, with milk and salt, known as 'Dippity'.

BOXTY BREAD (Boxty in the pan)

1 lb. raw potatoes	1 lb. (2 cups) cooked mashed
1 lb. (4 cups) flour	potatoes
salt and pepper	4 oz. ($\frac{1}{4}$ cup) melted butter or
	bacon fat

Peel the raw potatoes and grate into a clean cloth. Wring them tightly over a basin, catching the liquid. Put the grated potatoes into another basin and spread with the cooked mashed potatoes. When the starch has sunk to the bottom of the raw potato liquid, pour off the water and scrape the starch on to the potatoes. Mix well and sieve the flour, salt and pepper over it. Finally add the melted butter or fat. Knead, roll out on a floured board and shape into round flat cakes. Make a cross over, so that when cooked they will divide into farls. Cook on a greased baking sheet in a moderate oven (300° F. electric; gas regulo 3) for about 40 minutes. This quantity will make about four cakes. Serve hot, split in two with butter.

BOXTY PANCAKES

Use the same ingredients with the addition of 1 teasp. bicarbonate of soda and enough milk to make a batter of dropping consistency. The pan or griddle is greased lightly and spoonfuls at a time are cooked over a moderate heat, on both sides. Served with butter, and sometimes sprinkled with sugar.

Co. Donegal, 1879–80

TEA BRACK

Winifred Abbe, Co. Offaly (c. *1900*).

A simplified version of the traditional yeasted Barm Brack (*see* page 69). The following quantities make three loaves for tin size 8 in. by 4 in. and 3 in. high.

1 lb. (3 cups) sultanas	1 lb. (3 cups) raisins
1 lb. (2⅓ cups, firmly packed) brown sugar	3 cups milkless tea, or ½ tea and ½ Irish whiskey

Soak the fruit and sugar in the tea overnight. (My grandmother used half tea and half whiskey, which made her bracks very popular with the gentlemen.)

The next day, add alternately:
1 lb. (4 cups) flour and 3 beaten eggs
Finally, 3 level teasp. baking powder. If a spiced brack is liked, add the same (3 teasp.) of mixed spices.

Turn into three greased loaf tins (size as above), and bake for 1½ hours in a moderate oven (300° F. electric; gas regulo 3). When cool, brush the top with melted honey to give it a fine glaze.

BUTTERMILK SCONES

Margaret Saunders, Carrick-on-Suir, Co. Tipperary (b. 1875).

Lisdoonvarna is the best known spa in Ireland, and the place has a very gay atmosphere. There are three springs: the Gowlaun (sulphur with traces of lithium), which is good for rheumatism and arthritis; the Twin Wells (sulphur and iron); and the Rathbaun, containing iron and a small quantity of manganese.

½ pt. (1 cup) buttermilk
10 oz. (2½ cups) flour

2 teasp. ammonium bicarbonate powder [1]
salt

Dissolve the ammonium bicarbonate in two tablesp. of buttermilk, then mix the flour into the rest of the buttermilk until a soft dough is formed. Add a good pinch of salt and the ammonium bicarbonate, and mix very well. Turn out on to a floured board or table, roll lightly and cut into 2-in. scones. Put on to a lightly greased baking sheet and bake in a hot oven (400° F. electric; gas regulo 5) for 15 minutes. Serve hot, split with butter. Makes twelve.

Ammonium bicarbonate can be used in place of baking powder, and in the same quantity for small cakes or buns. Anyone over a certain age may remember the evocative ammonia smell coming from the kitchen on baking days. The results are light, crisp buns, but the bicarbonate must *first be dissolved* in liquid before adding to the flour.

[1] Always used before the introduction of patented baking powder, and much more effective as it does not induce that rough feeling behind the teeth that some baking powders do. There is no taste of ammonia, as the heat of the oven in baking causes the ammonium bicarbonate to break down and diffuse away, leaving no residue, such as is left when bread soda or baking powder is used. It can be bought at any chemist.

Twin Wells (sulphur and iron), Lisdoonvarna, Co. Clare, c. 1908

PICKLED OR SOUSED HERRINGS

'Thim's not company fish!' ('*The Boat's Share*', Experiences of an Irish R.M. *by E. Œ. Somerville and M. Ross), but very good nevertheless.*

2 herrings per person	1 teasp. pickling spice
2 bay leaves	vinegar and water to cover
1 large sliced onion for 8 fish	salt and pepper

Clean the fish and remove the heads and tails. It is not necessary to fillet them. Lay them in an oven-proof dish, after rubbing a little salt into the skin. Add the bay leaves, pickling spice, the thinly sliced onion and pepper and barely cover the fish with a mixture of half vinegar and half water. Cover with a piece of oven foil or a lid and bake in a moderate oven (300° F. electric; gas regulo 3) for 30–40 minutes. Leave to get cold in the liquid. They are also served cold, with a little of the tangy liquid poured over. Also for mackerel.

Rostrevor, Co. Down, c. 1890

DUBLIN CODDLE

Traditionally eaten on Saturday night as a supper dish. It has been popular since the eighteenth century.

This savoury stew of bacon and sausages combines two foods known since the earliest Irish literature. Bacon (tinne or senshaille) is mentioned many times in the medieval Vision of MacConglinne, *as are sausages, particularly one called Maróc, and another called Indrechtán. Leeks and oatmeal were no doubt used in the earliest form of Coddle, but, since the eighteenth century, potatoes and onion have supplanted them.*

---

8 ($\frac{1}{4}$ in. thick) ham or bacon slices
4 large onions, sliced
4 tablesp. chopped parsley

2 lb. potatoes, peeled and sliced
1 qt. (4 cups) boiling water
salt and pepper
8 pork sausages

Boil the sausages and bacon or ham (cut into large chunks) in the boiling water for 5 minutes. Drain, but reserve the liquid. Put the meat into a large saucepan (or an oven-proof dish) with the thinly-sliced onions and potatoes and the chopped parsley. Season to taste, and add enough of the stock to barely cover. Lay greaseproof (wax) paper on top and then put on the lid and simmer gently, or cook in a slow to moderate oven (200° F. electric; gas regulo $\frac{1}{2}$–1) for about an hour or until the liquid is reduced by half and all the ingredients are cooked but not mushy. Serve hot with the vegetables on top and fresh soda bread and glasses of stout or Guinness.

SPICED TONGUE

If you kiss the Blarney Stone you will have a golden tongue or 'the gift of the gab'. Hence the term 'none of your blarney'. Until a few years ago one was lowered down the side of the castle to kiss the stone; nowadays you lie down and put your head over the side, and the operation is not so risky. Blarney Groves and Blarney Lake are very beautiful. The latter contains a notable red trout which is worth asking for.

The best tongue to use is a salted ox or calf tongue. In Ireland, tongue is often served cold after being pressed, but this spicy sauce was common in the late nineteenth century.

1 tongue (soaked in cold water overnight)	1 tablesp. aspic powder
1 large onion stuck with 4 cloves	sprig of thyme and parsley
	pepper

Trim a certain amount of the horny part off the tongue, but leave enough to ensure that the stock jellies. Add all the ingredients, then cover with cold water and simmer, covered, for about 4 hours, or until it is tender. Remove from the stock and plunge into cold water; this makes the skinning of the tongue very much easier. Skin and trim the tongue, and, if serving cold, curl it in a circle and put into a basin or dish. Taste the stock to see that it is not too salty, then strain off about 2 cups and boil up with 1 tablesp. aspic jelly powder. Pour this around and over the tongue and when cool put a plate on top and a weight to press it down. Slices can be cut off when cold. They should be thick and heated up in the following sauce:

½ cup redcurrant jelly	1 tablesp. freshly grated horse-radish
finely grated rind and juice of 1 lemon and 1 orange	1 cup tongue stock, mixed with 1 cup red wine or port
1 teasp. dry mustard powder	
2 tablesp. tarragon vinegar	

Boil all ingredients together for about 30 minutes; it will have reduced and become 'sticky'. A whole hot tongue can be served with this sauce, in which case double the quantities.

YEASTED FRUIT LOAF

Traditional; known in Ireland as Fruit Pan.

Ireland is famous for the excellence and variety of her home-made breads. Every farmhouse and many city dwellers regularly make Irish Soda Bread (see page 59), and, for special occasions, yeast loaves.

Traditional recipes vary but this is a well-tried and tested one. It makes two loaves for tin size 9 in. by 5 in. and 3 in. high. If a plain loaf is preferred, omit the fruit.

2 oz. (2 cakes) yeast
½ pt. (1 cup) warm potato water or water (105° F.–115° F.)
8 level tablesp. sugar
¼ lb. (½ cup) butter or margarine

2 eggs
2 tablesp. (¼ cup) lukewarm mashed potatoes
1 lb. 5 oz. (5¼ cups) approx. unsifted flour
5 oz. (1 cup) seedless raisins
1 teasp. salt

Cream the yeast in the warm potato water: then add the mashed potatoes, 2 tablesp. sugar and 1 cup or 4 oz. flour. Mix well until it is smooth, cover with a cloth and leave to rise in a warm place for about 30 minutes. Stir again, then add the rest of the sugar and another cup of flour. Beat until smooth. Now add the beaten eggs and the butter or margarine, melted, but not so hot that it would kill the yeast. Put in the raisins, the remaining flour and the salt and mix to make a soft dough. Knead for about 5 minutes, then put into a greased bowl, turning once. Cover again as before and leave for 1 hour. With the knuckles, punch it down and leave for 5 minutes. Divide into two and shape to size of tins, then put into the greased tins, cover and leave in a warm place until it has doubled in bulk, about 35–40 minutes.

Bake in a moderate to hot oven (350° F. electric; gas regulo 4) for 50–60 minutes. Test with a skewer if in doubt. When properly cooked, the loaf will have a hollow sound when tapped at the bottom.

Ladies shopping from their carriages, Dublin, 1888

POTATO CAKES

Traditional.

'. . . While I live I shall not forget her potato cakes. They came in hot, and hot from the pot oven, they were speckled with caraway seed, they swam in salt butter, and we ate them shamelessly and greasily, and washed them down with hot whiskey and water' ('The Holy Island', Experiences of an Irish R.M.—E. Œ. Somerville and M. Ross).

The three-legged iron pot is the origin of the term 'to take pot-luck'. In country districts it is used for roasting, stewing and for making cakes and bread. In counties Limerick and Cork it is also called a bastable oven, and the bread made in it a 'bastable cake'. Glowing turf (peat) sods are put on top when baking or roasting is being done to ensure even heat. The pot can be raised or lowered by a chain, and three short feet enable it to stand at the side of the hearth.

---

2 cups self-raising flour
2 heaped tablesp. butter or other fat
1½ cups mashed potato
¼ cup milk
caraway seeds (optional)
salt

Mix butter into the flour and add a good pinch of salt. Then mix in the mashed potato and pour in the milk to make a soft (not slack) dough. Roll out on a floured board and cut into rounds about 3 in. across. Sprinkle a few caraway seeds on top of each cake and bake in a hot oven (450° F. electric; gas regulo 6–7) for 20–30 minutes. Eat them hot, split across the middle and spread with butter. This dough can also be used to line a savoury flan tin. Makes about nine cakes (*see also* page 37).

Irish kitchen, about 1888

SAUCE PIQUANTE

Michael Kelly (b. Cork c. 1790), afterwards composer and director of music at the Theatre Royal, Drury Lane, London, and Italian Opera, 1822.

1 tablesp. capers	6 filleted anchovies
1 tablesp. dry mustard	3 hard-boiled egg yolks
1 tablesp. chopped parsley	½ pt. (1 cup) gravy from roast
1 tablesp. vinegar	lamb, or the same of melted
2 tablesp. olive oil	butter
1 chopped shallot	a pinch of cayenne pepper

Pound together the capers and parsley, then add the mashed egg yolks and mustard. When well mixed, add the anchovies, well mashed, and stir in the oil, vinegar, cayenne and finely chopped shallot. When well pounded in a mortar, stir it into the hot gravy or melted butter and serve with roast lamb, chops or cutlets. It is also good with veal or pork in which case use the appropriate gravy or melted butter. It is served hot. Makes approximately 2 cups.

SAUCE for Boiled Tripe, Calf's Head, Boiled Tongue or Pig's Trotters

Michael Kelly

1 teasp. each of brown sugar, dry mustard and black pepper (freshly ground) mixed together and added to 1 tablesp. garlick (sic) vinegar. When well blended it is stirred into ½ pt. (1 cup) melted butter.

CHEESE SAVOURY

The Countess of ClanWilliam, Montalto, Ballynahinch, Co. Down (c. 1900).

½ lb. (2 cups) grated cheese such as Cheddar
3 tablesp. milk
1 teasp. made English mustard
2 tablesp. chopped mixed pickles or chutney

2 tablesp. beer
4 oz. (½ cup) butter
4 large rounds of hot buttered toast
pepper

Grate or cut the cheese into small cubes and put into a saucepan with the milk, butter and beer. Stir over a low flame until the mixture is creamy. Then add the made mustard, pepper to taste and, when well mixed, the chopped pickles. Serve at once on rounds of hot buttered toast.

CHOCOLATE SANDWICH CAKE

This cake is unusual in that it contains mashed potato. This makes it hold the moisture and so prevents it becoming dry.

6 oz. (1½ cups) self-raising flour
6 oz. (⅔ cup) caster sugar
2 oz. plain chocolate, melted or 4 level tablesp. cocoa
½ teasp. salt

3 oz. (⅓ cup) cooked mashed potato
4 oz. (½ cup) butter
4 tablesp. milk
2 eggs

Cream the butter and sugar with the mashed potato, then add the melted chocolate or cocoa. Add the beaten eggs alternately with the flour and the salt. Finally pour in the milk, mixing well, to make a soft dropping consistency.

Well grease two 8 in. sandwich tins and divide the mixture equally between them. Cook in a moderate oven (400° F. electric; gas regulo 6) for 25–30 minutes. The top will be firm and springy to the touch when it is cooked. Let the cakes cool for a few minutes, then turn out on to a wire rack. The two sides are sandwiched together with whipped cream or chocolate icing.

YELLOWMAN

Near the Giant's Causeway is the town of Ballycastle, where on the last Tuesday in August a fair, lasting several days, is held. This is called Lammas Fair, and it has been held annually for over 350 years. Sheep and ponies are sold, and there are the usual fair-day delights. The two traditional foods are Dulse (see page 103) and Yellowman.

Yellowman is a toffee which has been made by the same family for several hundred years; it is a brittle yellow toffee, which is hammered off from large blocks. This is an original recipe.

1 lb. tin golden (corn or light) syrup

½ lb. (1 generous cup) brown sugar

1 teasp. baking soda

1 heaped tablesp. butter

2 tablesp. vinegar

Melt the butter and run it round the pan. Then add sugar, syrup and vinegar. Stir until sugar and all ingredients are melted. Boil without stirring until a little of the toffee becomes crisp and brittle if put in cold water. Then add the baking soda, which will make it foam up; stir again, then pour on to a greased slab or a large dish. Turn edges to the centre, and pull the toffee when cool enough. Pull until it is pale yellow in colour. It can be poured into a greased tin and cut into squares if preferred.

*'Did you treat your Mary Anne to dulse and yellowman
At the Ould Lammas Fair, at Ballycastle, O?'*

Giant's Causeway, Co. Antrim, c. 1860

Bacon, Eggs and Potato Cakes[1]

The bacon rashers should be trimmed of rind with a pair of scissors or a knife, put into a warm pan and cooked according to taste. Before adding the eggs, a little knob of butter should be added to the bacon fat, the bacon removed and kept hot and the eggs broken into the hot fat. The fat must not be too hot: that is, the eggs should just set as they are put in and not be allowed to frizzle and become brown round the edges. If the pan is tipped away from the cook and some of the hot fat taken up in a spoon and poured over the yolk, it will give a nice glazed appearance and result in the top being cooked at the same time as the bottom. When serving potato cakes the mixture should be made up before starting to cook the bacon and eggs. In fact, in Ireland it is usually cold cooked potato cakes that are heated up in the bacon fat. If Drisheen or black pudding is also served it is a typical Irish 'fry' (*see* page 79).

POTATO CAKES

Traditional.

2 cups freshly mashed potatoes	4 tablesp. flour
2 tablesp. melted butter or bacon fat	salt

Mash the potato well, add the fat and then work in the flour. Salt to taste and turn on to a floured board. Roll out to a $\frac{1}{2}$-in. thickness and cut into rounds or triangles. Cook in a lightly greased pan for 3 minutes on each side and prick with a fork while cooking (*see also* page 27). Makes approximately 20.

[1] Called Fadge in the north.

CREAMED FRESH HADDOCK

8 fresh haddock fillets	1 heaped teasp. made English
½ pt. (1 cup) half-cream and	mustard
half-milk	flour
4 oz. (½ cup) melted butter	salt and pepper

Dip the fillets in the seasoned flour, then roll them in the melted butter. Put them in a flat pan with any left over butter and add the milk and the cream. Heat gently and, when bubbling, reduce the flame, cover and simmer very gently for not more than 15 minutes or until the fish is cooked and the liquid reduced.

Remove the fillets to a warm serving dish and keep hot. Stir in the mustard to the sauce and reduce over a hot flame until it thickens slightly. Scrape round the edges so that all the essence is in the sauce. Pour over the fish and serve. It can be decorated with sprigs of parsley if desired. It is a simple dish, but one that enhances the full flavour of fresh good fish. Lemon wedges can be served but are not essential. This method can be used for any fillets of white fish, such as cod, hake, plaice, etc.

Cork harbour, c. *1860*

STUFFED PORK TENDERLOIN STEAKS

One of the most traditional cuts of meat in Ireland, which does not exist in English butchery, although now I think they are imported. It is a fillet of the pig and is lean and delicious.

Pork steaks can be roasted, grilled or casseroled. Before stuffing they must be prepared as follows: the steaks are slit along the length, down the centre, but not cut through. The two flaps are then pulled gently, so that the gap widens out. Then, with a sharp knife, it is scored down the length without cutting through the meat, so that when you have finished it presents a flattish, rectangular shape. They are now ready for stuffing.

2 pork steaks	2 tablesp. butter
1 cup water	

FOR THE STUFFING

2 cups fresh white bread-crumbs	2 tablesp. melted butter
1 teasp. each fresh chopped thyme and sage	finely grated peel and juice of $\frac{1}{2}$ lemon
1 medium onion	a pinch of mace
1 tablesp. chopped parsley	milk
	salt and pepper

Sprinkle the breadcrumbs with just enough milk to moisten them but do not make them sloppy; about $\frac{1}{4}$ cup should be enough. Add all the other ingredients and mix well. Some cooks add an egg to the stuffing, but in my opinion this hardens it too much. There are two ways of stuffing pork steaks, both equally good. The first method is to lay the stuffing on one flattened steak, cover with the other and secure with skewers or twine. The other way is to roll up the steak with the stuffing, so that you have short chunky rolls which are then secured with skewers or twine. Whichever way is chosen, they are then rubbed with butter and lightly seasoned, then put into a roasting pan if they are being roasted, or in a casserole if being braised. 1 cup of water is added to the roasting pan, it is covered with oven foil and roasted in a moderate to hot oven (350° F.–400° F. electric; gas regulo 4–5) for about 1 hour. They can be turned half way and basted. The addition of an unpeeled but quartered orange to the liquid is not traditional, but gives a marvellous sweetness to the pork. The gravy is reduced over a hot flame, or thickened as desired. Pork steaks are good either hot or cold.

For braising, the stuffed steaks are put into a casserole, with stock or water added and finely sliced root vegetables. Again, a little grated orange peel gives a fine flavour. The lid is put on and it is cooked in a slow to moderate oven (275° F.–300° F. electric; gas regulo 2–3) for about $1\frac{1}{2}$ hours.

Gresham Hotel, Sackville Street (now O'Connell Street), Dublin, 1904

WILD DUCK

Charlotte Mason, from The Lady's Assistant, *published Dublin, 1778.*

Wild duck, widgeon (slightly smaller) and teal (the size of a young pigeon) are plentiful in Ireland. In County Limerick it used to be traditional to cook these birds with juniper branches or berries.

Juniper bushes grow wild in many parts of Limerick. The finest wild duck is the mallard. It should be hung for at least two or three days before cooking, when a greenish tinge on the thin skin of the belly will be noted. This does not mean that it is bad; it is correct. Contrary to prejudiced opinion, wild ducks do not taste fishy; indeed it would be surprising if they did, as their diet consists of the plant life in lakes and estuaries.

One wild duck is a good meal for two people, at the most three, so it is advisable to cook two, as it is delicious cold. This eighteenth-century recipe uses a chafing dish, but it can just as easily be done in a roasting tin.

2 wild duck	½ pt. (1 cup) red wine
1 orange or lemon	salt and pepper
4 tablesp. butter	

The original recipe says: 'To eat wild duck, widgeon, to perfection. Half roast them; when they come to the table, slice the breast, strew on pepper and salt; pour on a little red wine and squeeze the juice of an orange or lemon over; put the gravy to this; set the plate over the lamp, cut up the bird, let it remain over the lamp till enough, turning it.'

I do it the following way:

Rub the butter over the birds and roast them in a moderate oven (350° F. electric; gas regulo 3–4) for 20 minutes. Then add the red wine, orange or lemon juice, salt and pepper and continue cooking for 10–15 minutes. Put the birds on to a warmed dish and keep hot, then reduce the gravy on top of the stove on a brisk flame. A dash of brandy does no harm if you are feeling extravagant. Thin crisp fried potatoes should be served, and a lettuce salad with some peeled orange slices mixed in it and an olive oil and vinegar dressing.

Enniskerry, Co. Wicklow, c. 1867

BAKED ONIONS

This recipe has the same effect as a boiled onion.

These are cooked country style, as they were when large ovens were on the go all day and night. Very good when eaten with chops or steaks or with potato oaten cakes; known in the country as 'Pratie Oaten'.

1 large onion per person   a little water

Put the onions in a baking tin, unpeeled, with about 1 in. of water, not more. Bake in a slow to moderate oven (250° F.–275° F. electric; gas regulo 1–2) for 1½–2 hours or until they are soft when you squeeze them. To eat, the brown skin is pulled back and cut off at the root and the onion is eaten with salt and pepper and a pat of butter. One of the most delicious ways of serving onions.

PRATIE OATEN

2 cups warm mashed potatoes   1 cup (approx.) fine oatmeal
½ cup melted butter   salt

Work enough fine oatmeal into the potatoes to form a dough which is fairly soft. Add salt and enough melted butter or good bacon dripping to bind it. Scatter plenty of oatmeal on a board and roll out the dough. Cut into shapes and either cook on both sides on a hot greased griddle in the oven, or fry in a little bacon fat on top of the stove. Serve hot. They are very good for breakfast with bacon, eggs and sausages. Makes approximately 15.

COD'S ROE RAMKINS

Cod's roe is a traditional breakfast dish in Ireland. The cooked roe is cut into half-inch slices and fried in bacon fat on both sides. It is delicious eaten with rashers of bacon. This recipe comes from the turn of the century and makes a light luncheon dish with salad.

It is better to buy roe raw and cook it yourself. Do not choose too large a roe; the smaller ones have a more delicate flavour.

Wrap the roe in a piece of cheesecloth and put it into warmed salted water. Let it cook very gently—the water should just bubble and no more—for at least 30 minutes. When cooked, take it out and let it get cold. The outer membrane is taken off before using, but leave it on until you use the roe, as it keeps it moist.

½ lb. cooked cod's roe
2 cups loosely packed fresh breadcrumbs
2 eggs, separated
a pinch of mace
¼ cup of cream
juice of ½ a lemon
1 tablesp. chopped parsley
salt and pepper

Mash the roe and mix with breadcrumbs, mace and seasonings. Add the parsley and lemon juice and the beaten egg yolks mixed with the cream. Leave for 10 minutes until the breadcrumbs have absorbed all the moisture, then add the stiffly beaten egg whites. Put either into individual greased dishes or one big one and bake in a hot oven (400° F. electric; gas regulo 5) for about 15 minutes for the small ones and 30 minutes for the large one, or until they have puffed up and are golden brown. Serves 4.

Kingstown (now Dun Laoghaire) Pier, 1858

HONEY MOUSSE

County Wexford is famous for the excellence of its honey. It has a unique flavour, and is delicious slightly warmed and served with pancakes and a squeeze of lemon.

1 lb. jar of honey   4 eggs, separated

Separate the white from the yolk of the eggs and then mix the egg yolks with the liquid honey. (If the honey is 'set' and thick, stand the jar on a piece of wood in warm to hot water until it liquefies.) Cook on a very low heat, stirring all the time, or preferably in a double boiler, until the mixture thickens like a custard. Remove from the stove and let it cool. Whisk the egg whites until stiff and fold into the mixture. Pour into either individual dishes, or one dish, and chill. It should be left for several hours before serving.

BEEF BRAISED WITH ONIONS, CARROTS AND GUINNESS [1]

Originally porter was used for this stew, but half Guinness and half water makes a good rich dish.

2 lb. boned stewing steak (shin of beef has the best taste)	3 bay leaves
	2 tablesp. flour
	2 tablesp. cooking oil or fat
1 large onion	1 tablesp. chopped parsley
$\frac{1}{2}$ lb. carrots	$\frac{1}{4}$ pt. ($\frac{1}{2}$ cup) Guinness
1 cup soaked prunes and hazelnuts (optional)	$\frac{1}{4}$ pt. ($\frac{1}{2}$ cup) water
	salt and pepper

Trim the meat and cut into convenient serving pieces; do not make them too small. Heat the oil or fat and put in the bay leaves. Let them crackle, but put the lid on, for they jump and spatter the oil. Then add the beef and fry on both sides; when half done, add the sliced onion and let that gently colour to pale gold. Sprinkle the flour over and let it brown, then add the Guinness and water. A little more liquid may be needed, in which case make it water or stock to just cover the meat. Season to taste and add the parsley and carrots cut into circles. Put the lid on and braise in a slow to moderate oven (275° F.–300° F. electric; gas regulo 1–2) for about 2 hours. Stir it around at least once and add a little more liquid if it is in danger of drying up.

In the nineteenth century, soaked and stoned prunes (about 1 cup), stuffed with grilled hazelnuts, were added half an hour before the meat was ready. They make a marvellously rich garnish. As with all casseroles, the dish is better if cooked, allowed to get cold and then very gently re-heated. Serves 4.

[1] This dish is sometimes served in France, and called '*ragoût à l'Irlandaise*'.

The Dublin to Ballybrack coach, setting off from the Shelbourne Hotel, St Stephen's Green, Dublin, 1904

TROUT BAKED IN WINE

J. O'Brien, Co. Clare (c. 1880).

4 trout (1 per person)	$\frac{1}{4}$–$\frac{1}{2}$ bottle white wine
4 oz. ($\frac{1}{2}$ cup) butter	$\frac{1}{2}$ lemon
2 tablesp. chopped parsley	salt and pepper

Mix the chopped parsley into half the butter and then divide into four pats. Put one pat into each cleaned fish, then place them in an oven-proof dish and rub salt and white pepper into them. Pour the wine around, cover and cook in a moderate to hot oven (350° F.–400° F. electric; gas regulo 4–5) for 20 minutes. Add the rest of the butter cut into small pieces and the juice of the lemon. Cover again and cook for another 10 minutes.

It can be served hot or cold; if the latter, chill and it will be a soft jelly. If served hot, cauliflower sprigs are excellent with this dish. In eighteenth- and nineteenth-century Ireland, the florets were cooked in a little milk to barely cover, with a knob of butter and salt and pepper. The liquid almost evaporates and gives the cauliflower a very good flavour.

IRISH STEW

Traditional.

One of the Irish dishes which are known all over the Western world. It was originally made with either mutton or kid (no farmer would be so foolhardy as to use his lambs for it), potatoes and onions. The pure flavour is spoilt if carrots, turnips or pearl barley are added, or if it is too liquid. A good Irish stew should be thick and creamy, not swimming in juice like soup.

3 lb. best end of neck chops, trimmed of fat, bone and gristle
2 lb. potatoes
1 lb. onions

1 tablesp. chopped parsley and thyme, mixed
$\frac{3}{4}$ pt. water (2 cups approx.)
salt and pepper

Cut the meat into fairly large pieces and see that the fat, bone etc. is trimmed off. Peel and slice the potatoes and onions. Put a layer of potatoes in a pan, then herbs, then sliced meat and finally onion. Season each layer well and repeat this once more, finishing with a thick layer of potatoes. Pour the liquid over, cover with a sheet of foil, then the lid, and either bake in a slow oven (250° F. electric; gas regulo 1–2) or simmer very gently on top of the stove, shaking from time to time so that it does not stick, for about 2 hours. Add a very little more liquid if it seems to be getting very dry.

Another method is to place the trimmed neck chops around the inside edge of a saucepan, and put the sliced onions and small potatoes with herbs and seasonings in the middle. Add the water, put on the lid and then cook very slowly for about 2 hours until the meat is quite tender. If the meat is so placed, you will have no difficulty in serving.

Sherlock Holmes and Dr Watson investigating the Dillon Place Mystery, Dublin, 1891

BROTCHÁN FOLTCHEP [1]

Traditional leek and oatmeal soup. For many centuries oatmeal, milk and leeks were the staple diet of the Irish. Here they are combined to make a substantial soup. Legend has it that St Patrick tended a dying woman, who said that she had seen a herb in the air, and would die unless she ate it. St Patrick said to her: 'What is the semblance of the herb?' 'Like rushes,' saith the woman. Patrick blessed the rushes so that they became a leek. The woman ate it afterwards, and was whole at once.

6 leeks (large)	2 tablesp. flake oatmeal
1 heaped tablesp. butter	2 pts. (4 cups) milk or stock
1 tablesp. chopped parsley	salt and pepper

Wash the leeks thoroughly to remove grit. Leave on the green part and cut them into chunks about 1 in. long. Heat up the liquid with the butter and when boiling add the oatmeal. Let it boil, then add the chopped leeks and season to taste. Put the lid on and simmer gently for 45 minutes. Add the parsley and boil again for a few minutes.

For nettle brotchán use 4 cups young nettle tops, packed tightly. Wear gloves when picking them and cut with scissors. A little cream can be added if liked.

[1] Brotchán is the Irish for broth, and this soup made with young nettle tops was a favourite dish of the great St Colmcille.

Trim, Co. Meath, c. 1900

IRISH SODA BREAD

Traditional.

Irish soda bread is one of the specialities of the country and is still baked in countless farmhouses and homes all over Ireland. It is made in white or brown loaves, the latter being made from whole-wheat flour. It is very easy to make.

WHITE

1½ lb. (6 cups) plain flour   1 teasp. bicarbonate of soda
½ pt. (1 cup) buttermilk, sour   1 teasp. salt
    milk, or fresh milk; if the
    last, 1 teasp. cream of tartar
    is added to dry ingredients

Mix all the dry ingredients together in a basin and make a well in the centre. Add enough milk to make a thick dough. Stir with a wooden spoon; the pouring should be done in large quantities, not spoonful by spoonful. The mixture should be slack but not wet and the mixing done lightly and quickly. Add a little more milk if it seems too stiff. With floured hands put on to a lightly floured board or table and flatten the dough into a circle about 1½ in. thick. Put on to a baking sheet, and make a large cross over it with a floured knife. (This is to ensure even distribution of heat.) Bake in a moderate to hot oven (375° F.–400° F. electric; gas regulo 5) for about 40 minutes. Test the centre with a skewer before removing from the oven. To keep the bread soft, it is wrapped up in a clean tea-towel. This quantity will make 1 large loaf or 2 small ones.

BROWN

Exactly the same as above, but use 1 lb. (4 cups) whole-wheat flour and ½ lb. (2 cups) plain white flour. A little more milk is used to mix the dough.

If a brittle texture is required add 1 tablesp. of melted butter to the above quantities.

The bread should not be cut until it is quite cold and 'set'. This takes from 4 to 6 hours.

Sultanas (about ½ cup) are sometimes added to the dough, and a favourite with children is Treacle Soda Bread. It is made as white soda bread, but 2 tablesp. of black treacle (molasses) is heated with the milk and 1½ tablesp. of sugar is added to the dough.

Classically, soda bread should be cooked in a bastable oven, with glowing turf sods on top to give all-round heat. Because of this, in parts of west Cork soda bread is called Bastable Cake (*see* page 27).

The Miller's family, Co. Roscommon, c. 1857

OCEAN SWELL JELLY [1]

Chondrus crispus is a branching mucilaginous seaweed, which grows on many coasts in Europe and North America. It is dark purple or green when growing, but when dried it is bleached and called Irish Moss, or Sea-Moss. Owing to its gelatinous quality it is used as a vegetable gelatine and makes excellent jellies, aspics, beverages and even breads and pastries. The rich vitamin content makes it an ideal food substance and the prepared form is obtainable in most health food shops.

$\frac{1}{2}$ cup (packed tightly) carrageen
1 egg white
$\frac{1}{4}$ pt. ($\frac{1}{2}$ cup) cream

2 oz. (2 heaped tablesp.) sugar
1 pt. water
peel of 1 lemon, or vanilla flavouring if preferred

Steep the carrageen in water to cover for 10 minutes, and then drain. Simmer for 25–30 minutes in 1 pt. of water with the sugar and lemon peel. Strain and let it cool slightly. Meanwhile, whip the egg white stiffly and combine with the cream, also whipped. Mix with the carrageen liquid and gently heat up to just under boiling point. Pour into a wetted mould and chill. Turn out mould to serve, and decorate with fresh fruit slices.

For blancmange, use milk instead of water and omit the egg white. The soaked carrageen liquid is used for mixing pastry or dough.

[1] Ocean Swell is the brand name of a prepared carrageen.

Ocean Swell, Co. Galway, c. 1910

COCKLE SOUP

Cockles are members of the Cardium family, and there are over two hundred varieties. They are small bivalves with radial shell markings. Many of the 'cockles' used in Ireland, and exported to France at an alarming rate, are first cousins and members of the clam family (Venerupis decussata). They are called locally, in Co. Kerry, where they are extensively fished, Carpetshell and Kirkeen, and in Irish, Ruacan. They have a smooth surface with a slight ridge running vertically over the shell.

Small clams, mussels or scallops can be used for any of these recipes, or a mixture of all four shellfish.

4 doz. cockles	2 tablesp. chopped parsley
2 heaped tablesp. butter	½ cup chopped celery (optional)
2 heaped tablesp. flour	cream to taste (approx. ½ cup)
2 pts. (4 cups) cockle stock	salt and pepper
1 pt. (2 cups) milk	

Scrub the cockles well, to get rid of the sand and grit. Then put them into a large saucepan, with preferably sea-water, to cover. If this is not available use salted water. Bring them to the boil, when they will open. Do not continue cooking once the shells are open but cool until cold enough to handle and then take the cockles out of their shells. Melt the butter in a saucepan, stir in the flour, then add the strained cockle juice and milk, stirring all the time until it is smoothly blended. Put in the chopped parsley, celery and seasoning and cook for 10 minutes. Finally add the cockles, heat and serve with a little cream on each portion.

BOILED COCKLES in County Down are cooked as above, and when taken from their shells are heated up with butter, pepper, salt and the juice of a lemon.

COCKELTY PIE; cooked as for soup, a little grated onion added and covered with a pastry crust (*see* page 77 or 89) which is baked in the oven for 30 minutes and served hot.

'Cockles and mussels alive, alive Oh!' Dublin, 1904

PORK OR LAMB CISTE

Traditional Irish dish, nowadays found only in private homes. An excellent winter meal and much easier than making a pie.

6 pork or lamb chops, trimmed of fat, but with the bones left in
3 pork kidneys, or ½ lb. pig's liver or lamb equivalent
2 medium onions

1 large sliced carrot
1 pt. (2 cups) approx. stock or water
1 tablesp. chopped parsley
½ tablesp. chopped thyme
1 bay leaf
salt and pepper

FOR THE CISTE

8 oz. (2 cups) flour
4 oz. (1 cup) grated suet
½ cup (approx.) milk for mixing

½ cup sultanas (for pork only)
1 teasp. baking powder
½ teasp. salt

Put the prepared chops around the inside edge of a medium-sized saucepan with the bone ends sticking up and the chopped kidneys or liver, sliced carrot, onions and herbs in the centre. Season well and add enough water or stock to barely cover the vegetables, etc. in the middle. Put the lid on and simmer gently for about 30 minutes. Then taste, and adjust seasoning if necessary. During this time make the ciste by mixing the flour, suet, baking powder and salt to a stiffish dough with the milk. Add a little more if it seems too thick. It should be the consistency of pastry. Put on to a floured board and gently roll to the exact size of the top of the saucepan. It is then pressed down to meet the stew and, in the case of lamb, the bones should be pressed through it. Cover with a tight lid, seeing that the dough does not come to within an inch of the top, to allow for rising, and cook over a gentle heat for 1–1½ hours.

It is served by loosening the ciste with a knife around the edge, then cutting into wedges, about six of them. These are placed around a deep dish and the stew is put in the middle. Each portion should consist of a wedge of ciste, a chop, kidney or liver and vegetables. If the chops are very small, the quantities should be doubled.

Ciste can be cooked in a moderate oven for the same length of time if preferred. Serves 6 to 8.

COLCANNON

Traditionally eaten in Ireland at Hallowe'en or All Hallows' Day on 31st October, the vigil of Hallowmas or All Saints' Day. It is thought originally to have been a Druidic festival, and the two chief characteristics of ancient Hallowe'en were the lighting of bonfires to honour the Sun-God in thanksgiving for the harvest and the belief that it was the one night in the year during which ghosts and witches were most likely to walk abroad. It was also a Druidic belief that Saman, the Lord of Death, summoned together the evil souls that had been condemned to inhabit the bodies of animals. Indeed in parts of Ireland it is known in Irish as Oiche Shamhna, 'the vigil of Saman'. From this name also comes 'sowans'; the inner husks of oats after winnowing and threshing, which are allowed to ferment in salted water, drained, and the liquid is boiled up and eaten like porridge. Another traditional food is Barm Brack (see page 69).

Colcannon should correctly be made with kale, but is more often made with cabbage. A plain gold ring, a sixpence, a thimble or a button are often put into the mixture. The ring means you will be married within a year; the sixpence denotes wealth, the thimble a spinster and the button a bachelor, to whoever gets them.

1 lb. each of kale or cabbage, and potatoes, cooked separately

2 small leeks or green onion tops

1 cup milk or cream

4 oz. ($\frac{1}{2}$ cup) approx. butter

salt, pepper and a pinch of mace

Have the kale or cabbage cooked, warm and well chopped up while the potatoes are cooking. Chop up the leeks or onion tops, green as well as white, and simmer them in milk or cream to just cover, until they are soft. Drain the potatoes, season and beat them well: then add the cooked leeks and milk.

Finally blend in the kale, beating until it is a pale green fluff. Do this over a low flame and pile it into a deep warmed dish. Make a well in the centre and pour in enough melted butter to fill up the cavity. The vegetables are served with spoonfuls of the melted butter. Any leftovers can be fried in hot bacon fat until crisp and brown on both sides.

Leap Castle, Co. Offaly. The most haunted house in Ireland: reputed to have twenty-four ghosts. An O'Carroll castle

BARM BRACK

Traditional. Eaten all the year round, but particularly at Hallowe'en (see Colcannon, page 67), when it has a gold ring baked in it; whoever gets the ring will be married within a year. Barm is the old word for yeast; for an unyeasted brack, see Tea Brack, page 15.

1 lb. (4 cups) flour	3 oz. ($\frac{3}{4}$ cup) caster sugar
$\frac{1}{2}$ pt. (1 cup) tepid milk	$\frac{3}{4}$ oz. (1 cake) yeast
$\frac{1}{2}$ lb. ($1\frac{1}{4}$ cups) sultanas	4 oz. (1 cup) currants
2 heaped tablesp. butter	2 oz. ($\frac{1}{2}$ cup) mixed chopped
$\frac{1}{2}$ level teasp. ground cin-	candied peel
namon	$\frac{1}{4}$ level teasp. nutmeg
$\frac{1}{2}$ level teasp. salt	1 egg

All utensils should be warm before starting to make a brack. Sift the flour, spices and salt together, then rub in the butter. Cream the yeast with 1 teasp. of the sugar and 1 teasp. of the tepid milk. It should froth up; if it doesn't, it means the yeast is old and stale. Add the rest of the sugar to the flour mixture and blend well. Then pour the tepid milk and the beaten egg on to the yeast mixture, and combine with the flour, etc. Beat well with a wooden spoon or turn into the warmed bowl of an electric mixer and work with the dough hook at speed 6–8 for about 5 minutes. The batter should be stiff but elastic. Fold in the dried fruit and chopped peel; cover with a cloth and leave in a warm place until the dough is twice the size. Turn out and divide into two portions. Grease two 7-in. cake tins and put one portion in each tin, adding the ring at this stage. Cover again and leave to rise for about 30 minutes. Bake in a moderate to hot oven (400° F. electric; gas regulo 5–6) for about 1 hour. Test with a skewer before taking out of the oven. Glaze the top with 1 tablesp. sugar dissolved in 2 tablesp. boiling water and put back in the hot oven for about 3 minutes. Turn out to cool on a wire tray and when cool serve in slices with butter. It keeps very well, but if it gets stale it is very good toasted and served with butter.

Lady Gregory of the Abbey Theatre always brought a Barm Brack from her house, Coole Park, Co. Galway, which was handed around with tea in the Green Room. It was particularly a 'barm' after the uproar on the first night of J. M. Synge's *The Playboy of the Western World*.

Children playing on Leinster House lawn, Dublin, 1904

CHAMP

Traditional potato dish, particularly in the northern counties.

'*This mighty monarch . . . . is no other than the three-legged iron pot, who has done such good service for so many generations, and will continue to do so if properly treated by his subjects.*'

Alexis Soyer, 1854.

1½ lb. (2½ cups) freshly cooked hot mashed potatoes

4 tablesp. melted butter (approx.)

salt and pepper

10 spring onions, scallions or 2 leeks, cooked in ½ cup of milk

Cook the chopped spring onions, green part as well as white, in the milk; drain, but reserve the milk. Mash the potatoes, season to taste, then add the spring onions. Beat well together and add enough hot milk to make the dish creamy and smooth. Put into a deep warmed dish, make a well in the centre, and pour the hot melted butter into it. The dry potato is dipped into the well of butter when serving.

Champ can also be made with chopped parsley, chives, young nettle tops and freshly cooked young green peas. In the latter case the peas are kept whole and added last. For a supper dish, scrambled eggs are often served in the well in the centre. Sprinkled with chopped parsley, it makes an attractive dish.

The following traditional rhyme was prompted by the heavy wooden pestle or beetle, which was used to mash large wooden tubs full of potatoes, in the days when they were the main food of many Irish people.

There was an old woman
who lived in a lamp
she had no room
to beetle her champ.
She's up with her beetle
and broke the lamp
and then she had room
to beetle her champ.

Ancestral home of President William McKinley (25th President of United States from 1896 to 1901), Dervock, Co. Antrim, c. 1900

DUBLIN BAY PRAWNS

These succulent little creatures are not a prawn at all, but the Norway lobster (Nephrops norvegicus). *They are often mis-named scampi, which are a variety of the Norway lobster, found in the Adriatic Sea, and of a larger size. The Dublin Bay prawn gets its name in a curious way. About one hundred and fifty years ago, when all the fishing boats were sailing ships, and there was no refrigeration to speak of, all shellfish caught in the nets were cooked and eaten straight away, as they would be dangerous to eat if kept. They became the 'perks' of the crew and their womenfolk on board. Sailing ships of all nationalities used to anchor in the waters of the Lambay Deep, a sheltered spot off the coast of County Dublin, in the vicinity of Lambay Island, before setting sail to fish their way home. All the freshly caught shellfish would be cooked by the women, who would sell them in the streets of Dublin as 'Dublin Bay prawns'. Whatever they got for them would be spent on themselves—probably on stout or linen. In fact they occur in most of the colder waters of the European Continental Shelf, and as they breed all the year round they are always in season.*

Freshly caught Dublin Bay prawns should be cooked in as simple a way as possible so that the delicate flavour is not absorbed. Use the frozen ones for Prawn Cocktail, or for putting in batter and deep frying.

2 lb. Dublin Bay prawns

3 oz. (3 heaped tablesp.) butter

juice of 1 lemon

salt

Steam the prawns over boiling water for 15–20 minutes, then leave them to cool. Shell them by removing the head and tail, then pinching the belly part of the shell, which will crack easily and come in two. Melt the butter in a frying-pan and turn the prawns in the hot butter, sprinkle lightly with salt and finally add the lemon juice, turning it all together. The butter will become a faint coral pink and the delicate flavour of the prawns be preserved.

Kingstown (Dun Laoghaire), 1904

LIMERICK HAM

Limerick ham is rightly famous all over the world. In the eighteenth century the characteristic flavour of the smoked ham was obtained from juniper berries, which grew freely in the county. They were also used in the cooking of wild duck in Limerick. The following recipe for smoking ham comes from a family manuscript of 1779.

'When you take your hams out of the pickle, and have rubbed them dry with a coarse cloth, hang them in a chimney, and make a fire of oak shavings and lay over it horse litter [straw] and one pound of juniper berries. Keep the fire smothered down for two or three days, and then hang them up to dry.'

All smoked hams should be soaked overnight in cold water, drained and then boiled for 20–25 minutes to the pound in cold water to cover, with a heaped tablesp. brown sugar, pepper and a pinch of mace. When cooked, the brown skin should be removed and, if serving boiled, the fatty layer covered with a mixture of half breadcrumbs, half brown sugar and a good pinch of ground cloves. It can then be baked in a moderate oven for 30–40 minutes with a cupful of the ham stock, if a baked ham is preferred.

In County Sligo, when winter vegetables, particularly the green ones, were scarce, ham or bacon joints were cooked with watercress. The peppery flavour of watercress makes a good contrast with sweet ham or bacon, and slices about 1 in. thick can also be used.

Watercress 'cooks down' like spinach, so, despite its strong flavour, at least a pound of picked watercress should be used for 3–4 lb. ham. Cook the ham or bacon as above in cold water, and 45 minutes before it is ready add the watercress. When the meat is cooked, take it out and remove the skin, cover with breadcrumb, sugar and clove mixture, and put to 'set' the crust in a slow oven. Lift out the cress with a strainer, squeeze the liquid out, then chop it coarsely and arrange around the ham or bacon.

LEMON SAUCE

A suitable sauce for this dish is to melt 1 heaped tablesp. butter in a saucepan, add the same amount of flour, and, when well mixed, 1 cup of the hot ham stock. Stir until it boils and make sure there are no lumps. Finally add the grated peel and juice of 1 lemon, stir again and serve hot.

O'Connell Street, Limerick, c. 1890

WELLINGTON STEAK

A favourite of the Duke of Wellington. Excellent for those who like their steak underdone.

2 lb. fillet steak (tenderloin) in one piece

3 heaped tablesp. butter
salt and pepper

FLAKY PASTRY (rough)

$\frac{1}{2}$ lb. (2 cups) flour
$\frac{1}{2}$ teasp. salt
$\frac{1}{2}$ teasp. lemon juice
6 level tablesp. butter

6 level tablesp. lard
6 tablesp. iced water
1 egg for glazing

Cut the fats in small pieces lightly into the flour and salt. Make a well in the centre and add a little of the water and lemon juice to mix with the flour. Do not beat up the fats. Pour in enough of the liquid to make a fairly stiff dough, then put it out on to a lightly floured board. Fold it into three, like an envelope, and turn the open edge towards you. Roll it out, and repeat this four times. Leave to rest in a cold place for at least 30 minutes and longer if possible.

Season the fillet and rub with butter all over. Roll out the pastry so that it is large enough to wrap around the steak, moistening the edges with water so that they are secure. Bake in a hot oven (400° F.–425° F. electric; gas regulo 6–7) for 15 minutes, then glaze it with a mixture of 1 egg beaten with 1 tablesp. water, and bake for a further 10 minutes. If preferred, the steak can be cut into sections and rolled individually in the pastry.

The Wellington Testimonial, Phoenix Park, Dublin, c. 1867
(Erected by public subscription during the Duke of Wellington's lifetime)

DRISHEEN

Traditional name for a black or blood pudding in County Cork. It is larger in diameter than the usual black pudding. Cork men and women journey from many parts of the world to taste it again. Traditionally made from sheep's blood; nowadays pig's blood, and often pig's liver with it, is used. At home in Tipperary, marvellous puddings were made the same way from turkey or goose blood.

It is made from two parts blood (well salted to keep it liquid) to one part cream or full-cream milk, mixed together with a handful of breadcrumbs or oatmeal, pepper, a pinch of mace and a sprig of tansy. As tansy is a difficult herb to find today, thyme is often used. When made at home, and sausage casings are not available, the mixture is poured into bowls and either steamed or cooked in another pan of water in a moderate oven (300° F. electric; gas regulo 3) for about 1 hour. It can be eaten warm or left to get cold. Then it is sliced and either fried or grilled, for breakfast or supper, often with bacon, eggs and sausages.

TRIPE

Tripe is another country favourite. It is usually sold 'dressed', but cooks much more quickly if brought to the boil two or three times in fresh cold water before cooking.

1 lb. tripe	1 lb. onions
1 pt. (2 cups) milk	2 slices lean ham or bacon
2 tablesp. cornflour (cornstarch)	2 tablesp. chopped parsley
breadcrumbs	salt and pepper

Prepare the tripe as above, then cut into 2 in. pieces, together with the ham. Peel and slice the onions and combine with the tripe, ham and milk. Season well, cover, and simmer gently for about 2 hours, or cook in a slow oven for the same time. Dissolve the cornflour in a tablesp. of water, add, and let it boil up, stirring all the time. Add the parsley 5 minutes before serving, sprinkle the breadcrumbs on top and brown gently under the grill.

DUBLIN LAWYER

Traditional.

Uncooked lobster should be used for this dish. The fishmonger will prepare it for you, but see that the fish is alive first. It is dangerous to eat shellfish that has been dead for some time. It is killed by plunging a sharp instrument into the cross on the head.

1 fresh lobster, cut in two down the centre, lengthwise	3 heaped tablesp. butter
	4 tablesp. Irish whiskey
	salt and pepper
$\frac{1}{2}$ cup ($\frac{1}{4}$ pt.) cream	

Remove the meat from the tail of the lobster and also from the claws and head, but retain the shells. Cut it into chunks, heat the butter, but do not let it brown, then turn the raw lobster in it. Season to taste. Pour over the Irish whiskey which has been warmed, and set fire to it. Mix the cream with the pan juices, and let it just gently heat, but on no account boil. Put back into the half shells and serve hot.

It can be made with lightly cooked lobster, but the flavour is finer if cooked in the correct way.

Crab is excellent served the same way, but, if using crab, it can be cooked first. All shellfish should be cooked in *cold* sea or salted water brought to the boil. In this way the fish becomes faint and does not struggle. The flesh is tenderer as a result. Leave to cool in the water.

Eden Quay, Dublin, c. 1868

81

CRUIBÍNS

Traditional. Sometimes spelt, and also pronounced, crubeens, it is the Irish for pig's trotters. They used to be a great favourite in pubs on Saturday night, and can still be found in country districts. They are served with soda bread and stout.

The hind feet are the true cruibíns: they have more meat on them, the front feet being used to boil down for gelatine. Not an elegant dish, but delicious eaten in the fingers on certain occasions. They are sold already pickled, but not cooked, in pork butchers'.

12 pickled pig's trotters	A small bunch of mixed parsley
1 large carrot	and thyme
1 large onion	water to cover
1 bay leaf	salt and pepper

Put all ingredients into a large saucepan, bring to the boil, then simmer for about 2–2½ hours. They can be eaten warm from the pot, or cold, when they will be a thick jelly.

A modern refinement is to take the meat from the bones, after splitting the foot down the middle, and then roll them in beaten egg mixed with dry mustard powder (about 1 teasp. for 2 eggs) and finally dip them in breadcrumbs. They are fried in bacon fat on all sides, or heated under a moderate grill, and are delicious. Allow 2 per person.

A pig's trotter added to a stew of beef or pork makes it very rich and good. (For sauce, *see* page 29.)

OYSTERS

The finest oysters in Ireland come from the beds in County Galway. An oyster festival is held in Galway town each year to open the festival at the beginning of September. Generally speaking, on account of the high prices which they command nowadays, oysters are usually served on a plate in the half-shell, with cracked ice and home-made brown bread, and butter, cayenne pepper and lemon wedges on the side.

They are, however, very good if put into a light batter and fried in deep oil for a few minutes. Two or three put into a beef stew or a beef pudding gives an unforgettable flavour, and in the nineteenth century, when they were very cheap, excellent soups and soufflés were made with oysters.

FRIED OYSTER

12 oysters per person

BATTER FOR 2 DOZEN

1 cup flour	1 egg
1 cup milk	salt and pepper

Make the batter by beating the egg and adding it to the flour, salt and pepper. Beat in the milk gradually, seeing that the batter is smooth. Use an egg-beater or a whisk to get rid of any lumps. Leave the batter in a cool place for 30 minutes. Open and beard the oysters, then dip them in the batter and fry in deep hot, but not smoking, oil until they are golden brown. The oysters should not be too much cooked. Serve hot with lemon wedges and the oyster juice trickled over.

OYSTER SOUFFLÉ

1 doz. oysters or the equivalent tin	juice of $\frac{1}{2}$ lemon
	2 eggs
$\frac{1}{2}$ cup fresh white breadcrumbs	$\frac{1}{2}$ cup cream
	a pinch of mace, salt and pepper

Save the oyster liquor and add it to the lemon juice, then heat it and pour over the breadcrumbs. Chop the oysters and add to the crumbs, then mix in the cream. Separate the eggs, beat the yolks and add to this mixture, then season to taste. Finally add the stiffly beaten whites. Butter a basin or individual cups and put in the soufflé mixture, seeing that it does not come to 1 in. of the top, to allow for rising. Cover with buttered paper and steam for 1 hour, if in a large basin, or 40 minutes if in small ones. Turn out carefully and serve hot. Serves 4.

Selling oysters at the oyster market, Clifden, Co. Galway, 1900. Clifden is the 'capital' of Connemara

PIG'S LIVER CASSEROLE

Adam Hodgins, Nenagh, Co. Tipperary, b. 1883.

Pig's liver is of a high standard in Ireland, and when cooked in the following way it resembles goose liver.

1 lb. pig's liver
6 rashers bacon (streaky if possible)
1 large onion
a little flour

$\frac{1}{2}$ teasp. meat essence
1 tablesp. chopped parsley
1 cup water or stock
salt and pepper

Take the rind from the rashers, and lay two on the bottom of a casserole. Rub the liver slices (see that they are not too thin) in flour, then put half the sliced onion on top of the rashers, followed by a layer of liver. Repeat this until all the ingredients have been used up, ending with bacon rashers. Season very well between layers, add parsley, the stock or water, cover and cook in a moderate oven (350° F. electric; gas regulo 4) for no longer than $1\frac{1}{2}$ hours. The liver can be left in one piece if preferred, in which case cook for 2 hours. Serves 3 to 4.

IRISH CURD OR CHEESE CAKE

Adapted from the manuscript book of Catherine Hughes, Killinaule, Co. Tipperary, 1755.

Curds (gruth *in Irish*) *formed an extensive part of the diet of the ancient Irish. They are mentioned in the earliest documented sources. Various early cheeses were made from them, and it is possible that a cheese called* faiscre grotha *means literally 'pressed curd'. The Reverend R. H. Ryland in* The History, Topography and Antiquities of the County and City of Waterford, *1824, says: 'Cheese made from skimmed milk and called Mullahawn, was formerly an article of commerce in Waterford, and was exported in large quantities . . .'*

PASTRY

6 oz. (6 heaped tablesp.) flour
3 oz. (3 heaped tablesp.) butter
1 tablesp. sugar
$\frac{1}{2}$ teasp. salt
water

FILLING

$\frac{1}{2}$ lb. (2 cups) sweet curds or cottage cheese
2 eggs, separated
2 heaped tablesp. sugar (vanilla sugar if possible)
grated peel and juice of $\frac{1}{2}$ lemon
1 tablesp. butter

FOR THE TOPPING

1 egg and 1 tablesp. each of sugar, flour and melted butter

First make the pastry by mixing the fat into the flour, sugar and salt to a firm, pliable dough with a few tablesp. water. Cool if possible before using. Make the filling by well mixing the curds with the sugar, soft butter, grated peel and juice of the lemon and the beaten egg yolks. Beat it well, then add the stiffly beaten egg whites. Roll out the pastry to fit a flan-tin 7 in.–8 in. across, line the tin with it and paint the bottom with beaten egg (this prevents the bottom pastry becoming heavy).

Put the filling into the pastry case, and, using the rest of the egg, mix it with the topping sugar, melted butter and flour. Pour this evenly over the top. Bake in a moderate oven (350° F. electric; gas regulo 4) for 35–40 minutes, or until the top is golden brown. Serve cold, but not chilled, cut into wedges.

A handful of raisins or sultanas were sometimes added to the filling. It is a matter of taste: I prefer the simpler variety.

SPICED BEEF

Traditionally eaten in Ireland at Christmas, when it can be bought in all butchers' shops, sometimes tied with ribbon and decorated with holly. It is quite easy to spice beef at home, and preparations should begin one week before it will be used.

The following are the ingredients for spicing a 6-lb. joint:

3 bay leaves
1 teasp. cloves
6 blades mace
1 level teasp. peppercorns
1 clove garlic

1 teasp. allspice
2 heaped tablesp. brown sugar
2 heaped teasp. saltpetre
1 lb. coarse salt

For cooking the meat you will need:

1 6-lb. lean boned joint of
  beef
3 sliced carrots
½ pt. Guinness

3 medium sliced onions
a bunch of mixed herbs
1 teasp. each ground cloves
  and ground allspice

Rub all the dry ingredients together, then pound in the bay leaves and garlic. Stand the meat in a large earthenware or glass dish, and rub the spicing mixture thoroughly all over it. This should be done every day for a week, taking the spicing mixture from the bottom of the dish and turning the meat twice. Then wash the meat, and tie it into a convenient shape for cooking.

Sprinkle over about 1 teasp. each of mixed allspice and ground cloves, then put it into a large saucepan on a bed of the chopped vegetables. Barely cover with warm water, put the lid on and simmer gently for 5 hours. During the last hour add the Guinness.

It can be eaten hot or cold, but at Christmas it is usually served cold, in slices. If wanted cold, the meat should be removed from the liquid and pressed between two dishes with a weight on top.

Grand Hotel, Malahide, c. 1904

SOLE

There are two kinds of sole in Ireland: one is Lemon sole, a delicate, milky-tasting fish, and the other is a much 'meatier' game fish. The former should be eaten very fresh; the latter is all the better for being kept in a cool place for a few days. It gives it a wonderful flavour. In Ireland it is known as Black sole and is the same fish as Dover sole in England. In all cases the simpler ways of cooking are best, and they should be grilled or broiled rather than fried.

LEMON SOLE

1 fish per person, filleted in two halves	1 heaped tablesp. butter
1 tablesp. chopped parsley and chives, mixed	lemon wedges for serving
	salt and pepper

Put one fillet flat in the grilling pan, skin side down; season and spread over the chopped herbs and half the butter. Put the other fillet, skin side up, on top and spread the rest of the butter over. Grill on both sides, under a moderate heat. The milkiness of the fish mixes well with the herb butter.

BLACK SOLE

This is usually grilled 'on the bone' for flavour; the fish can be filleted afterwards if necessary, although it is an easy fish to fillet oneself. The black skin is removed by the fishmonger, who will take off the white one as well, if desired. Black sole vary from about 8 in. to 12 in. in length, and, as they are plump fish, a big one is a large meal for one person.

Rub the fish with salt 30 minutes before cooking, then add a little white pepper and well cover with butter. Grill on both sides and serve with a knob of butter which has been worked with chopped parsley and lemon juice: known in nineteenth-century Ireland as 'Hotel butter'.

Kingstown (now Dun Laoghaire) Pier, c. 1860

MARSHMALLOW CRACKERS

Cream crackers were invented and marketed by W. & R. Jacob & Co., in 1885, on the initiative of Mr George N. Jacob. Puff cracknels and marshmallow biscuits were brought out in 1897. The fame of the cream cracker has spread all over the world. They are eaten mostly with cheese and butter, but finely pounded they make a good topping for a savoury dish which is cooked in the oven. They have a saltier flavour than breadcrumbs. A simple way of using them, and popular with children, is the following:

20 cream crackers
20 small pats of butter

20 marshmallow cubes
20 almonds

Put a marshmallow on top of each cream cracker and a small piece of butter on the marshmallow. Press a blanched almond into the butter, then grill them under a moderately hot grill until the marshmallow has melted over the biscuit.

GRILLED MACKEREL WITH GOOSEBERRY SAUCE

Charlotte Mason, from The Lady's Assistant, *Dublin, 1778.*

4 cleaned and filleted mackerel
1 tablesp. butter
salt and pepper

FOR THE SAUCE

½ lb. gooseberries
2 tablesp. sugar
1 tablesp. butter
2 tablesp. chopped fennel

FOR THE STUFFING

4 heaped tablesp. breadcrumbs
1 tablesp. chopped parsley
2 egg yolks
grated peel of 1 lemon
pinch of nutmeg
salt and pepper

Mix all the stuffing ingredients together and put it inside the mackerel, then fold over and secure. Rub a little softened butter over, and broil (grill) gently on both sides until the fish is done.

Cook the gooseberries in ½ cup water with all other ingredients. Do not let them overcook, but just burst open. Serve hot.

The same sauce was also served with mackerel which has been poached in water, salt and lemon juice. Herrings can be cooked in the same way.

'By lorries along Sir John Rogerson's Quay', Export Guinness, 1904, Dublin

PLOVER OR WOODCOCK, BRAISED

'The Sportsman's breakfast: first, a large bowl of salmon soaked in vinegar – a very common dish this . . . and a bottle of Port wine.' From A Sportsman in Ireland *by A Cosmopolite, 1897.*

From a manuscript dated 1802.

4 plover
$\frac{3}{4}$ pt. (2 cups) stock
$\frac{1}{4}$ pt. ($\frac{1}{2}$ cup) white wine
1 blade of mace
1 tablesp. flour mixed with
   1 tablesp. butter, for thick-
   ening
salt and pepper
juice of $\frac{1}{2}$ a lemon

FOR THE STUFFING
4 hard-boiled egg yolks
4 artichoke bottoms
2 tablesp. chopped parsley
salt, pepper and a pinch of
   nutmeg

Mix the stuffing ingredients together and divide it amongst the four birds; put it into the body of each bird, then lay them in a casserole. Season them well, pour over the stock, wine and add the blade of mace. Cover and cook in a moderate oven (350° F. electric; gas regulo 4) for 35–40 minutes. Thicken with the flour rubbed in butter and finally add the lemon juice. Heat up before serving.

Small game birds such as the above are also very good rubbed with butter and grilled over a turf (peat) fire, for about 10 minutes. Charcoal will do if turf is not available.

Three gentlemen in the mountains, Co. Kerry, 1860

CORNED BEEF AND CABBAGE

Traditional.

Also called 'salt' beef, this beef is rubbed with coarse salt to a thickness of about $\frac{1}{4}$ in., then with brown sugar and 1 teasp. of saltpetre (this turns it red). The joint is put into a bowl and turned each day for about a week. The leanest cut is called silverside or tail end; brisket is a mixture of fat and lean. Pork is also put into this pickle and known as pickled pork. It is cooked the same way as the beef. Already salted meat can be bought from most butchers. It is advisable to soak the meat for at least 3 hours before cooking, so that the stock from the meat can be used for soup.

4 lb. corned beef	1 teasp. dry mustard powder [1]
1 large sliced carrot	sprig of thyme and sprig of
2 large onions, 1 stuck with	parsley
4 cloves	pepper
1 large cabbage or 2 small	cold water
ones	

Put the meat into a large saucepan with all the ingredients except the cabbage. Cover with cold water and bring to the boil; then skim off any scum. Cover and simmer very gently for $\frac{3}{4}$ of an hour, then put in the cabbage, trimmed and cut into quarters. Leave a little of the stump on, as this adds flavour. Cook the meat for 30 minutes to the pound and serve on a dish surrounded with the cabbage.

The stock makes excellent dried split-pea soup, either the yellow or green variety. When cold, remove any fat from the top and add 1 lb. split peas per 2 qts. (8 cups) stock. Cook fairly fast for about $1\frac{1}{2}$ to 2 hours, or until the peas become a purée. If soaked overnight they cook much faster. This pea purée can be cooked with pickled pork and used as a sauce.

---

[1] I am indebted to Mrs Sarah Kenny for telling me of the dry mustard powder. It has a magical effect: the beef is always tender and moist after using it.

DULSE, SLOKE AND WILLICKS

About a hundred years ago the lower slopes of Cave Hill were the scene of much merry-making on Easter Monday. People were brought up on ponies and there was dancing, drinking, thimble-rigging and the rolling of dyed eggs. The eggs were mainly dyed with the flower of gorse (whin) bushes. This custom has not entirely died out in the North of Ireland.

'*There was a good run in local poteen* (home-brewed spirit), *and also cockles and mussels from Greencastle Strand . . . and dulse and willicks.' From a contemporary newspaper.*

DULSE

(*Rhodymenia palmata.*) Also called dillisk and dillesk, it is a reddish-brown seaweed found on all coasts of Ireland. It is sold dried and can be eaten raw or added to fish or vegetable soup. To cook, it must be soaked for 3 hours in cold water, then simmered in milk for the same time with a knob of butter and pepper. It can be added to mashed potatoes for Dulse Champ, and is good with all meats or fish.

SLOKE

(*Porphyra laciniata*) or sea-spinach, is also found on rocks all over Ireland. It is called laver in England and Wales. Sloke should be simmered in water for 4 or 5 hours; drained, then dressed with butter, cream and a squeeze of orange or lemon juice. Excellent with roast lamb, boiled ham or fish.

WILLICKS or WILLOCKS

(*Littorina littorea.*) The local name for periwinkles or winkles. They are a small shellfish or sea snail. Winkles are boiled in their shells in cold sea-water for 10 minutes. Traditionally they are got out of their shells with a pin and dipped in fine oatmeal before eating.

Belfast Lough, c. 1913. Near to Cave Hill with caves and the earthwork of Mac Art's Fort

MICHAELMAS GOOSE

There is an old saying in Ireland that if you eat goose on Michaelmas Day (29th September) you will never want money all year round. At that time they weigh about 10 lb. and are very tender. Traditional Irish stuffing for goose is potato: this cuts the grease and absorbs the rich flavour.

1 10-lb. goose
goose giblets, cooked in salted water

FOR THE STUFFING

1½ lb. cooked potato	liver of the goose
1 medium chopped onion	1 tablesp. chopped parsley
½ cup diced salt bacon	1 teasp. chopped sage
salt and pepper	

Mix all the stuffing ingredients together and season very highly, then put it into the body of the bird and secure the vent. Put the bird into a roasting pan with 1 cup of the goose giblet stock. Cover the bird with foil and roast in a hot oven (400° F. electric; gas regulo 5) for the first half-hour, then lower the heat to 350° F. electric; gas regulo 4 and cook for 20 minutes to the pound. Baste at least twice during the cooking and add another cup of stock if it is running dry. Remove the foil for the last 15 minutes to allow the skin to crisp up.

In the eighteenth and nineteenth centuries onion sauce was always served with goose. The onions were cooked in half milk and half water with a slice of turnip to draw out the strength. When soft they were treated as follows:

ONION SAUCE

The cooked onions (as above) were mashed, mixed with a knob of butter, a pinch of nutmeg, pepper and salt and beaten until smooth—sometimes finished with a little cream. Nowadays apple sauce is more usual.

APPLE SAUCE

½ lb. of peeled and cored apples are cooked in ½ cup of water until tender. Then they are sieved or mashed and 1 heaped tablesp. butter, the same of sugar and a pinch of nutmeg and salt are added. It is reheated and served hot.

St Kevin's House, commonly called St Kevin's kitchen, Glendalough, Co. Wicklow, c. 1860

ROAST CHICKEN WITH BOILED HAM

In Ireland, roast chicken, or turkey, is invariably accompanied by boiled or baked ham. A couple of good slices are served with each portion.

1 chicken (about 4 lb.)   chicken dripping, or oil or butter
chicken giblets, cooked in
   2 cups water

FOR THE STUFFING

3 large slices of crustless   the liver of the chicken
   white bread $\frac{1}{2}$ cup milk (approx.)
2 tablesp. chopped parsley   a pinch of mace or nutmeg
1 level teasp. chopped thyme   salt and pepper
1 clove garlic or $\frac{1}{2}$ small
   onion

Soak the bread in the milk, adding a very little more if necessary. The bread should absorb the milk and not be wet. Add all the other ingredients, chopped quite small, mix thoroughly and season well. Put into the crop or body of the bird and secure with a skewer. Put the bird into the roasting pan and rub with dripping, oil or butter all over the breast and legs. Cover with foil and roast in a moderate oven (350° F. electric; gas regulo 4) for not more than $1\frac{1}{2}$ hours. It will only be dry if overcooked. Put on to a warmed dish. Strain the excess fat off and add 2 cups of the stock from the giblets. Season to taste and let it boil up rapidly on top of the stove until it has reduced and thickened slightly. Serve with Bread Sauce.

BREAD SAUCE

1 cup white breadcrumbs   1 pt. (2 cups) milk
6 cloves   1 medium onion
1 small bay leaf   1 knob butter
a pinch of mace   10 peppercorns
2 tablesp. cream   salt

Peel the onion and stick the cloves into it, then put into a saucepan with the milk, mace, bay leaf and peppercorns. Bring to the boil and then draw aside and let it infuse for about 30 minutes. Strain the milk and then add the breadcrumbs. Stir gently to let the breadcrumbs absorb the milk, then bring gently to the boil. Season to taste and finally add the knob of butter and the cream. Serve as soon as possible.

(For Boiled or Baked Ham *see* page 75.)

SCALLOP AND MUSHROOM PIE

8 scallops
$\frac{1}{2}$ pt. (1 cup) milk
4 tablesp. sweet sherry
1 heaped tablesp. butter
1 lb. (3 cups) approx. cold
   mashed potato

$\frac{1}{4}$ lb. mushrooms
1 heaped tablesp. flour
1 tablesp. chopped parsley
salt and pepper

Cut the cleaned scallops into half, but do not cut the red coral; simmer in the milk with salt and pepper to taste for 15 minutes. Strain, but reserve the milk. Melt the butter in a saucepan, add the flour and mix well, then gradually stir in the warmed milk, seeing that it is free from lumps. Add the mushrooms cut into pieces, the sherry and the scallops. Put into an oven-proof dish and cover the top with mashed potatoes. Dot with butter and bake in a moderate oven (350° F. electric; gas regulo 4) until the top is gently browned, about 20–30 minutes. Garnish with parsley. Soft roes can be added to the scallops if they are available. Serves 4.

Cobh, Co. Cork, c. 1890

OATEN HONEYCOMB

Roberta Colbert, Cloughjordan, Co. Offaly, b. 1884.

Oatmeal, milk and milk products have been used since the earliest days as food in Ireland, in both sweet and savoury ways. Many monastic settlements lived entirely on these foods (see also Brotchán Foltchep, page 57).

½ lb. (2 cups) flake oatmeal	3 eggs, separated
2 oz. (½ cup) ground almonds	2 tablesp. honey
1 pt. (2 cups) milk	2 heaped tablesp. raisins or the
3 heaped tablesp. sugar	grated rind of 1 lemon
a pinch of ground cinnamon	3 tablesp. melted butter

Bring the milk to the boil, sprinkle the flakemeal in, and cook slowly for about 15 minutes, stirring all the time. Leave to cool, then beat in one at a time the ground almonds, honey, sugar, raisins or lemon peel, cinnamon, melted butter and beaten egg yolks. Mix it all well and finally add the stiffly beaten egg whites. Put into a buttered bowl or basin, cover and steam over hot water for 1½ hours. Turn out and serve hot with warm melted honey or cream. It is more delicate in flavour if made with lemon peel.

West High Cross (tenth century), Clonmacnoise, Co. Offaly, c. 1860. Monastery founded in A.D. *547*

SALMON

'In the middle of the table are two glass flagons, each containing about a gallon of whiskey, and everyone proceeds to use, what are significantly termed (par excellence) "the materials".'

A Sportsman in Ireland *by A Cosmopolite, 1897.*

Salmon has long been prized in Ireland: it features in myth and legend, notably Fionn MacCumaill (Finn MacCool) and the salmon which had eaten the hazelnuts from the Tree of Knowledge and thus gave that knowledge to the first person who tasted it when cooked.[1] It was the pièce de resistance at banquets given by the Kings of Ireland, when it was cooked on a spit, after being rubbed with salt and basted with butter and honey. Irish salmon is sweeter than many other kinds. A remarkable spectacle of Galway town is to see the salmon, packed like sardines, lying in the shallows under Salmon Weir Bridge during the season.

BAKED SALMON WITH CREAM AND CUCUMBER

1 5-lb. salmon	$\frac{1}{2}$ pt. (1 cup) cream
3 heaped tablesp. butter	juice of 1 lemon
1 medium-sized cucumber	2 sprigs of parsley
salt and pepper	

Put the parsley in the cleaned gullet of the fish and rub the butter over the outside. Put the whole into a fireproof baking dish, season well and pour the cream around. Cover with foil and bake in a moderate oven (350° F. electric; gas regulo 4) for 10 minutes to the pound. Remove from the oven and add the peeled and cubed cucumber and the lemon juice. Baste well and put back in the oven, uncovered, for a further 15 minutes. Skin the fish before serving and pour over the sauce. The cucumber should still be a little crisp to act as a foil for the buttery salmon. It is excellent hot, but can also be served cold. Small cuts can be cooked in the same way, but should be left whole: a tail end is good for this method.

[1] Grilled salmon steaks served with cold butter pats mixed with pounded grilled hazelnuts is a discovery of mine which links the past with the present.

Killarney, Co. Kerry, c. 1860

SWEETBREADS AND BACON

Family recipe, Co. Tipperary.

1 lb. calf's or lamb's sweetbreads (calf's are larger)
½ lb. tomatoes or 1 tin
1 cup water or stock

1 lb. streaky bacon rashers
1 small onion
1 tablesp. chopped parsley
salt and pepper

Soak the sweetbreads in cold salted water for at least 30
minutes. Change the water, salt it and bring them to the boil.
Cook for 10 minutes. Strain and let them get cold, then remove
any skin or membrane. Take the rind from the rashers and
wrap each sweetbread in the bacon. (If the sweetbreads are not
all the same size, cut them accordingly.) Put into a lightly
greased, oven-proof dish, season well, add the small onion
finely chopped, the sliced peeled tomatoes and stock. Sprinkle
with the parsley and cook in a moderate oven (350° F. electric;
gas regulo 3–4) for 35–40 minutes. If any of the bacon is not
utilized, roll into curls and grill them. Use these crisp bacon
rolls as a garnish on top of the sweetbreads when serving.

BOOKMAKER'S SANDWICH

1½ lb. sirloin or fillet (tender-   made mustard
  loin) steak   butter
1 long fresh crusty loaf, such   salt and pepper
  as a Vienna

Slice the loaf in half lengthways and butter it. Grill the steak according to taste, but do not overcook it. Trim off any gristle or fat when it is cooked and put it, warm, into the sliced bread. Season to taste and spread with mustard if liked. Put the top on and press down. Wrap in greaseproof (wax) paper or foil and put a light weight on top. When cold, cut downwards into fairly thick but biteable slices and put back into foil. The juices from the meat should absorb into the bread and so keep it moist. This gargantuan sandwich is often taken to race-meetings, or on shoots.

Punchestown Races, c. 1856

IRISH COFFEE

Blackchurch Hotel is now called Blackchurch Inn, and still very much the same to look at outside. Punchestown Racecourse is 'first on the left'.

Although of recent origin, this is all set to become a tradition. An excellent end to a meal, or a 'pick-me-up', as there is both 'ating and drinking in it'. Irish coffee is served in all restaurants, and most pubs, all over Ireland.

1 double measure Irish whiskey	1 cup strong, hot, black coffee
1 tablesp. double cream	1 heaped teasp. sugar

First of all warm a stemmed whiskey glass. Put in the sugar and enough hot coffee to dissolve the sugar. Stir well. Add the Irish whiskey to fill within an inch of the brim. Now this is the tricky part: hold a teaspoon curved side up *across* the glass and pour the cold cream slowly over the spoon. Do not attempt to stir the cream into the coffee. It should float on top and the hot whiskey-laced coffee is drunk through the cold cream.

Slainte 'gus Saol agat!   *Health and long life to you!*

Blackchurch Hotel (now Blackchurch Inn) on the way home from Punchestown Races, Co. Kildare, c. 1860

INDEX